# 12 INCREDIBLE FACTS ABOUT THE
# D-DAY INVASION

by Lois Sepahban

12 STORY LIBRARY

www.12StoryLibrary.com

12-Story Library is an imprint of Peterson Publishing Company and Press Room Editions.

Produced for 12-Story Library by Red Line Editorial

Photographs ©: Hulton-Deutsch Collection/Corbis, cover, 1; Library of Congress, 4, 15; Harris & Ewing/Library of Congress, 5; AP Images, 6, 7, 13, 17, 21, 28; Nehez/US Army Center of Military History, 10; US Army Center of Military History, 11, 25, 29; Bettmann/Corbis, 12, 19, 24; Berliner Verlag/Archiv/picture-alliance/dpa/AP Images, 14; National Archives/U.S. Army Center of Military History, 16; US Maritime Commission/Library of Congress, 18; Wall/U.S. Army Center of Military History, 20; Imperial War Museum, 22; Harry Harris/AP Images, 26; Dick DeMarsico/Library of Congress, 27

**ISBN**
978-1-63235-128-9 (hardcover)
978-1-63235-171-5 (paperback)
978-1-62143-223-4 (hosted ebook)

**Library of Congress Control Number: 2015933983**

Printed in the United States of America
Mankato, MN
October, 2016

Go beyond the book. Get free, up-to-date content on this topic at 12StoryLibrary.com.

# TABLE OF CONTENTS

# WORLD WAR II RAGES ON AFTER FIVE YEARS

At the beginning of 1944, the United States was in the midst of World War II. In the war, the United States allied with main world powers Great Britain, France, and the Soviet Union. They were called the Allied Powers. They fought against the Axis Powers, composed of Germany, Italy, Japan, and some smaller countries.

The war had been raging since 1939. That year, Germany invaded Poland. Poland's allies, France and Great Britain, declared war on Germany. Within a year, Germany invaded Denmark, Norway, Belgium, the Netherlands, Luxembourg, and France.

At first, the United States avoided the conflict. Then, on December 7, 1941, Japan bombed the US naval base in Pearl Harbor, Hawaii. The next day, the United States declared war on Japan. Because Japan and Germany were allies, Germany

A bomb explodes on the USS *Shaw* during the Japanese attack on Pearl Harbor.

## ADOLF HITLER

Adolf Hitler was the leader of the Nazi Party in Germany. In 1933, he became the leader of Germany. In 1939, Hitler ordered German troops to invade Poland. This invasion started World War II.

declared war on the United States three days later.

By 1944, the Allied Powers believed the only way to defeat Germany was to invade Europe. They hoped to start by freeing France, which was occupied by Germany. So the invasion would begin in France.

The Allied forces called their invasion plan D-Day. In order for D-Day to

# 5

## Number of years the world was at war before D-Day.

- The main Allied Powers were the United States, Great Britain, France, and the Soviet Union.
- The main Axis Powers were Germany, Italy, and Japan.
- The United States entered the war in 1941.

work, they needed four things to happen. First, they needed a good location. Second, they needed good weather. Third, they needed a full moon and low tide. Finally, they needed the element of surprise.

People in Washington read about the invasion of Poland in 1939.

# VETERAN GENERAL EISENHOWER TAKES COMMAND

In 1943, President Franklin D. Roosevelt appointed General Dwight D. Eisenhower commander of the Supreme Headquarters Allied Expeditionary Force. The Force was made up of British, US, Canadian, French, Polish, and Norwegian troops. Eisenhower would be in charge of D-Day.

Eisenhower was a good choice for many reasons. First, the invasion force would be made up of US, British, and Canadian troops. It was important that the commander get along well with everyone. Those who worked for Eisenhower respected him. He was known for supporting teamwork.

Eisenhower also had experience leading air, land, and sea invasions. D-Day would need all three.

Eisenhower's headquarters were in Great Britain, just outside of London.

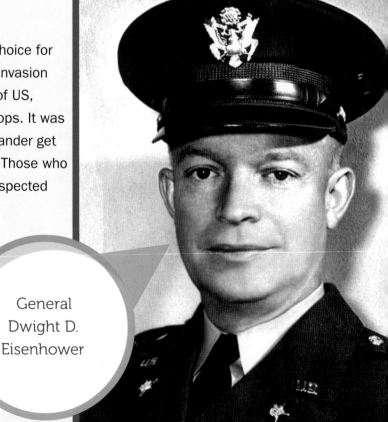

General Dwight D. Eisenhower

# 75

**Percent of Allied Expeditionary Force troops that were American.**

- Eisenhower would command the D-Day invasion.
- Most Allied soldiers respected Eisenhower.
- Eisenhower had experience leading air, land, and sea invasions.

In the months leading up to D-Day, he worked hard. By 6:00 a.m. every morning, he was out with the troops. He spent the day inspecting them and checking their training. He rarely slept for more than four hours at night.

Eisenhower talks with US soldiers on D-Day.

# NORMANDY IS PRIME SPOT FOR INVASION

Eisenhower and his advisors looked at several different locations as possible landing sites. They wanted the location to be close to Germany. They also wanted it to be close enough to Great Britain that planes could fly there without having to refuel.

That left them with few options. Holland, Belgium, and northern France were closest to Germany. But they were also the most heavily guarded. Other possible sites had natural barriers such as rivers, making them difficult to attack.

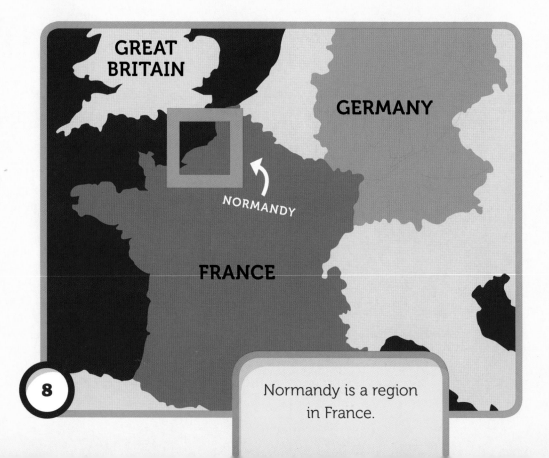

GREAT BRITAIN

GERMANY

NORMANDY

FRANCE

Normandy is a region in France.

# D-DAY BEACHES

**UTAH (US)**

**OMAHA (US)**

**GOLD (BRITISH)**

**JUNO (CANADIAN)**

**SWORD (BRITISH)**

**FRANCE**

Each country focused on different beaches.

General Eisenhower and his advisors chose the Calvados coast in Normandy, France. It had many advantages. There was a small port and airfield nearby. The beaches were wide and flat. And best of all, the Germans did not expect an invasion there.

## 50

Length, in miles (80 km), of the Calvados coast in Normandy.

- The Allies considered Holland, Belgium, and northern France for the invasion.
- The Calvados coast had wide, flat beaches.
- For the invasion, the beaches were divided and named.

The Allies divided the beach into five landing zones. Beginning in the east, the zones were Sword Beach, Juno Beach, Gold Beach, Omaha Beach, and Utah Beach. British troops would invade Sword Beach and Gold Beach. Canadian troops would handle Juno Beach. The Americans were in charge of the invasion on Omaha Beach and Utah Beach.

# BAD WEATHER DELAYS D-DAY

General Eisenhower's weather forecasters said that the best days for an invasion were June 5, 6, and 7. Those were the only three days in June 1944 when the tide was low and the moon was full. A low tide would help soldiers avoid mines on the beaches. A bright full moon would help pilots see. Eisenhower planned for D-Day to take place on June 5.

On June 4, a storm began moving in. Forecasters predicted storm clouds would cover the moonlight. Strong winds and rough waves would be a problem for the paratroopers and landing craft.

Eisenhower worried about changing the date. The element of surprise was important. Every day wasted gave German spies time to discover

On June 1, soldiers get ready for D-Day by loading weapons into landing crafts.

## OPERATION OVERLORD

The Allied invasion of France was first called Operation Overlord. It is sometimes called D-Day. In military language, "D-Day" is the day when a combat operation begins. So D-Day for Operation Overlord was June 6, 1944.

US troops march through British streets on their way to the docks on D-Day.

the plan. But in the end, Eisenhower decided to delay the invasion.

Later that night, forecasters predicted a short break in the bad weather. Beginning on June 5, the weather would calm down for about 36 hours. That would give the Allied invasion force just enough time to drop paratroopers after midnight on June 6. It would also give them time to get their landing craft in position. Then troops could land on the beaches in the morning on June 6. Eisenhower made a decision: D-Day was on for June 6, 1944.

## 500
Number of weather stations in Great Britain that reported the weather to Eisenhower and his staff.

- There were only three days in June 1944 when the tide was low and the moon was full.
- Allied commanders worried that every day the invasion was postponed gave the Germans a better chance to discover their plans.
- D-Day was delayed by one day.

## THINK ABOUT IT

Do you think Eisenhower's decision to postpone D-Day was an easy decision? Why or why not? Using information from these pages, make a list of the things Eisenhower considered when making his decision.

# SECRET MESSAGES SENT TO FRENCH RESISTANCE

In order to help the D-Day invasion succeed, the Allies needed assistance from French Resistance fighters. These fighters were French men and women. They fought against the Germans occupying their country.

For D-Day, Eisenhower and his advisors gave the French Resistance fighters an important job. While the D-Day troops were landing by sea and air, French Resistance fighters had to sabotage infrastructure. They had to destroy bridges and railroads. This would make it difficult for the Germans to get fresh troops to fight the Allied invaders.

The Allies told the French Resistance fighters of these plans through secret messages. The messages appeared in newspapers and radio broadcasts. Another popular way to send messages was by pigeon. One spy would put a secret message inside a tiny tube attached to the pigeon's leg. Then the pigeon flew to the next spy who would be able to read the message and report back.

At 6:30 p.m. on June 5, Eisenhower's staff sent a secret radio message: "It is hot in Suez."

French Resistance fighters speak with a US officer.

German officers and soldiers sit at a Paris café during Germany's occupation of France.

# 2

**Number of secret radio messages that announced the D-Day attacks to French Resistance fighters.**

- French Resistance fighters lived in German-occupied France.
- Eisenhower's staff sent secret messages to French Resistance fighters.
- French Resistance fighters helped by attacking bridges and railroads.

Another secret radio message followed it: "The dice are on the table." This told the French Resistance fighters to start their sabotage work.

## THE WRONG MESSAGE

The Allies wanted to trick the Germans so that they wouldn't know when or where the Allies would attack. Sometimes they sent messages to France that gave wrong information on purpose. The Allies hoped the Germans would believe the messages.

# GERMANY RIDDLES THE COAST WITH PERILS

German Field Marshall Erwin Rommel was in charge of the defenses along the coast of Normandy. This area was called the Atlantic Wall. Fortifications had been built along the coastline. It stretched from the Bay of Biscay west of France to the Arctic Ocean. It was nearly 3,000 miles (4,800 km) long.

By June 1944, the Atlantic Wall consisted of concrete and steel towers on land. The towers had long-range guns that could shoot toward land or sea. In the water, metal, wood, and concrete were used to make obstacles. Each obstacle had mines strapped to it. If anything touched the mine, it would explode.

The beaches were also fortified. Barbed wire stretched across the Atlantic Wall. At least five million land mines were buried in the sand. To guard against paratroopers

Bunkers were part of the Atlantic Wall.

Allied soldiers practice for D-Day on a British beach.

# 6.5 million

**Approximate number of mines along the Atlantic Wall.**

- The Normandy coast was part of the Atlantic Wall.
- Troops on D-Day would have to be wary of the mines.
- Minesweepers would be part of the first wave on D-Day.

invading by air, Rommel had ordered the fields behind the beaches to be flooded. Booby traps and mines were spread out in the flooded areas.

Eisenhower and his advisors knew that the US, British, and Canadian troops would face these obstacles on D-Day. The area had already been scouted. Part of their invasion plan was to send minesweepers in first. The minesweepers would destroy as many mines as possible. Then the troops would begin their invasion.

# PATHFINDERS JUMP AT MIDNIGHT

On D-Day, the first part of the invasion plan was to send in paratroopers. Paratroopers are fighters who jump from an airplane with a parachute.

The first group of paratroopers was called pathfinders. The pathfinders' job was to mark drop zones. Drop zones show other airborne troops safe places to land. This job was dangerous. The sky was cloudy, making it difficult for them to know where to jump. German troops shot at their planes. The pilots had to zigzag around to avoid them.

At 12:15 a.m., the first pathfinders jumped from their planes. They began landing one minute later. Most of the pathfinders landed off course. They had one

US paratroopers get ready to board their planes.

# 120

### Number of pathfinders on D-Day.

- Pathfinders jumped at 12:15 a.m.
- Pathfinders' job was to mark drop zones.
- The drop zones would give the next wave of paratroopers safe places to land.

## THE 101ST AIRBORNE

Shortly after 1:00 a.m. on D-Day, 13,000 paratroopers from the 101st Airborne began jumping over drop zones. Their job was to destroy Atlantic Wall fortifications. Then Allied troops would begin landing on the beaches. The paratroopers faced many dangers, including German machine guns and the flooded and booby-trapped fields.

hour to mark the drop zones. Airborne troops would begin their jumps at 1:15 a.m.

By 12:21 a.m., the first drop zone was marked. They used lights and radar beacons to mark the zones. Seven men held lights and lined up in the shape of a T. But they wouldn't turn on their lights until the first Allied plane was spotted overhead.

US paratroopers prepare to jump.

# "HITLER'S BUZZ SAW" RIPS HOLES IN LANDING CRAFT

At dawn on June 6, Allied bombers began flying over the landing zones. They would drop bombs on the Atlantic Wall defenses. When the bombers looked down from the sky, they saw that the ocean was filled with hundreds of landing craft.

At around 5:30 a.m., troops loaded onto landing craft. These small boats were designed to carry troops from the giant naval ships to the beaches. Landing craft had a flat bottom. This made it easier to unload troops. But it also made the boats difficult to steer in the choppy waves. The landing craft were heavy too. Many flooded and sank, forcing troops into the ocean to swim and walk to shore.

When landing craft off Omaha Beach were approximately

An aerial view shows Allied troops and landing craft arriving on the beaches of Normandy, France.

A German machine gun team

400 yards (366 m) from shore, German guns began firing on them. Mortar shells and machine gun bullets shot holes in the landing craft. The machine gun was nicknamed "Hitler's buzz saw" because of the zipping sound its bullets made. It could fire 1,200 bullets per minute. Troops forced into the water had heavy equipment strapped to them. Many drowned. Many who didn't drown were killed by German machine guns. It would take the troops almost three hours to reach the end of the beach.

## 156,000
### Number of Allied troops that landed in Normandy.

- Hundreds of landing craft approached the beaches.
- On Omaha Beach, troops faced heavy machine gun fire.
- Some troops drowned when their landing craft was destroyed.

## SEASICKNESS

In order to give troops a memorable last meal, a large breakfast was served just before the invasion. Bouncing on the choppy waves in landing craft, many US troops became seasick. Seasickness weakened some soldiers. These soldiers were more likely to be hurt or killed on D-Day.

# TROOPS AT UTAH BEACH LAND OFF COURSE

Utah Beach was the westernmost landing zone. It was on the Cotentin Peninsula. The large port of Cherbourg was also on the Cotentin Peninsula. The Allies needed this port to land their ships.

The invasion of Utah Beach began just after midnight on June 6 with pathfinders. But the airborne teams who followed them sometimes had trouble finding the drop zones. Clouds covered the sky. In spite of this, most of the 13,000 paratroopers made it to their meeting points.

At 6:30 a.m., the first wave of sea landings began. The ocean current was moving south. The landing craft were difficult to steer. Because of this, the landings were more than 500 yards (457 m) south of where they were supposed to be. Still,

US troops arrive on Utah Beach.

within half an hour, the first troops had made it onto the beach and over the dunes beyond it.

By 7:45 a.m., the Americans had pushed the Germans past the shoreline. And by 8:30 a.m., the only Germans left at Utah Beach were prisoners of the Americans.

All day, US troops fought the Germans for control of the Cotentin Peninsula. They fought in villages, including in houses and churches. By nightfall they met their first goal: the troops who had landed by sea met up with the airborne troops.

# 4,414

Tonnage of bombs dropped by US bombers on Utah Beach on D-Day.

- Airborne teams at Utah Beach struggled to find their landing zones.
- Landing craft faced strong winds and landed off course.
- Troops at Utah Beach were successful in taking German prisoners.

German prisoners on Utah Beach

# SOME TANKS ATTACK, OTHERS SINK

The Allies wanted the heavy firepower of a tank to take out the fortifications of the Atlantic Wall. But getting a tank onto the beach would be a challenge.

At the end of World War I, the British began developing a floating tank. The version used at D-Day was called the Duplex Drive tank, or DD tank. It was made from a land

The DD tank had a canvas that could be pulled up around it when it was in the water.

## BANGALORE TORPEDO

The DD tank was one of many weapons used on D-Day. The Bangalore torpedo was a more helpful weapon. It was a metal pipe filled with explosives. The pipe could be linked to other pipe. On D-Day the long weapon was used to explode a path through barbed wire. The Bangalore torpedo is still used in war zones today.

tank. A flotation screen made of waterproof canvas was attached to the tank. It had a propeller that was hooked up to the tank's engine.

There were eight tank battalions on D-Day. They spread out along the five landing zones. The DD tanks were designed to be launched approximately two miles (3.2 km) from the shore.

On their way to the shore, tanks were at risk of sinking. They might run into mines. Some of the tanks landed safely. But on Omaha Beach, 27 of the 29 tanks sank in rough waves. After that, landing crafts began taking the tanks all the way to the shore. The tanks that did make it to land gave important help to the troops on the beaches. These strong weapons could damage the Atlantic Wall.

## 5
### Number of DD tanks a landing craft could carry.

- DD tanks were made from land tanks.
- At Omaha Beach, 27 of the 29 DD tanks never made it to shore.
- Some tanks were taken all the way to shore on landing crafts.

## THINK ABOUT IT

Do you think using the DD tanks on D-Day was a good idea? Write a paragraph explaining your argument. Use evidence from these pages to support your viewpoint.

# BRUTAL BATTLE FOR OMAHA BEACH LASTS 18 HOURS

At 6:30 a.m., the first wave of troops began landing on Omaha Beach. Their goal was to clear the five draws, or roads, leading from the beach through the cliffs.

As soon as troops reached the beach, they immediately dropped to the ground to crawl across the beach. The draws were approximately 300 yards (274 m) away. Between the troops and the draws were mines and barbed wire. Above them were gun towers. German machine guns began firing at the troops on the beach. Many soldiers were killed. The troops had nowhere to hide. The support they were supposed to have had never arrived. Bombers did not blow up the

Soldiers crawl past a fortification on Omaha Beach.

## COMPANY A: THE SUICIDE WAVE

British naval officers called Company A the Suicide Wave because of the obstacles they would face at Omaha Beach. Within minutes of landing, 100 of the 155 Company A troops were dead. Most of the rest were injured.

# 3,700

**Estimated number of killed, missing, and wounded soldiers at Omaha Beach on D-Day.**

- Troops on Omaha Beach faced heavy fire.
- Troops fought to control the draws, or roads.
- By midnight, the Allies had control of all the draws on Omaha Beach.

beach obstacles. Navy guns did not blow up the gun towers.

For the next hour, small groups of soldiers slowly made their way to the bottom of the cliffs. At around 8:00 a.m., a group of 32 soldiers reached the top of one of the cliffs. By 9:00 a.m., the Americans were beginning to see progress. Five of

the twelve German towers had been defeated. Over the next five hours, 5,000 US troops reached the top of the cliffs. US troops fought Germans for control of the draws. Finally, around midnight, the last draw was open to US tanks.

As the Allies took Omaha Beach, more reinforcements were able to come in.

25

# D-DAY IS THE BEGINNING OF THE END OF THE WAR

D-Day was a costly win for the Allies. More than 4,400 Allied soldiers were killed during the invasion. Thousands of others were injured, missing, or taken prisoner. But the battle would prove to be the turning point of the war in Europe. By the end of the day on June 6, the Allies had secured all five landing zones. The next day, the invasion moved inland. The first goal was to get to Paris.

The Germans fought back, but the Allies were stronger. In August 1944, the Allies pushed the Germans out of Paris. The Germans' only choice was to retreat. The Allies followed. From December 1944 to January 1945, the Allies and Germany fought for control of northwest Europe. In February 1945, the Allies began their invasion of Germany.

Citizens of Paris hold up a US flag after the Allies liberate Paris.

# 453

Number of days between D-Day and the end of World War II.

- The D-Day invasion was a victory for the Allies.
- After D-Day, Allied troops continued to advance through France.
- Germany surrendered on May 8, 1945.
- World War II ended on September 2, 1945.

## THINK ABOUT IT

What do you think made D-Day a success for the Allies? Find evidence in this chapter to support your ideas.

In April 1945, Adolf Hitler committed suicide. Less than two weeks later, on May 8, 1945, Germany surrendered. The war in Asia would continue on for several more months. On August 10, 1945, Japan surrendered. World War II finally ended on September 2, 1945.

A crowd of people in New York City's Times Square celebrate the end of World War II.

**September 17, 1939**
Germany invades Poland.
World War II begins.

**December 7, 1941**
Japan attacks the US naval base at
Pearl Harbor in Hawaii.

**December 8, 1941**
The United States declares war on
Japan. Germany declares war on
the United States three days later.

**December 6, 1943**
General Dwight D. Eisenhower is
appointed commander of the
Supreme Headquarters Allied
Expeditionary Force.

**June 4, 1944**
A storm delays D-Day by
one day.

**June 5, 1944**
Secret radio messages tell French
Resistance fighters to sabotage
infrastructure.

**June 6, 1944**
The Allies invade France on D-Day.

**August 1944**
The Allies push the Germans out of Paris.

**February 1945**
The Allies begin their invasion of Germany.

**May 8, 1945**
Germany surrenders.

**August 10, 1945**
Japan surrenders.

**September 2, 1945**
World War II ends.

# GLOSSARY

**advance**
To move forward.

**allies**
Two or more countries united for a common purpose.

**combat**
A fight between two groups or individuals.

**forecasters**
People who make predictions about what will happen in the future.

**fortification**
A structure built for defense.

**infrastructure**
The system of public works of a country.

**invade**
To enter in order to conquer.

**obstacle**
Something that stands in the way.

**paratroopers**
Troops trained to parachute from an airplane.

**radar beacon**
A device that emits a radar signal to identify a location.

**retreat**
To move away from a battle.

**sabotage**
To create a problem on purpose.

# FOR MORE INFORMATION

## Books

Atkinson, Rick. *D-Day: The Invasion of Normandy 1944.* New York: Henry Holt and Company, 2014.

Murray, Doug. *D-Day: The Liberation of Europe Begins.* New York: Rosen Central, 2008.

Platt, Richard. *D-Day Landings: The Story of the Allied Invasion.* New York: DK Publishing, 2004.

## Websites

BBC: Primary History
www.bbc.co.uk/schools/primaryhistory/world_war2

The National WWII Museum
www.nationalww2museum.org/see-hear/kids-corner.html

PBS: American Experience
www.pbs.org/wgbh/amex/dday

# INDEX

## About the Author

Lois Sepahban has written several books for children, including science and history, biography, and fiction. She lives in Kentucky with her husband and two children.

## READ MORE FROM 12-STORY LIBRARY

Every 12-Story Library book is available in many formats, including Amazon Kindle and Apple iBooks. For more information, visit your device's store or 12StoryLibrary.com.